Ferdinand Magellan

Betty Lou Kratoville

ORDER DIRECTLY FROM
ANN ARBOR PUBLISHERS LTD.
P.O. BOX 1, BELFORD
NORTHUMBERLAND NE70 7JX
TEL. 01668 214460 FAX 01668 214484
www.annarbor.co.uk

International Standard Book Number: 1-57128-169-X

9 8 7 6 5 4 3 2
0 9 8 7 6 5 4 3 2

Contents

CHAPTER 1

Magellan – The Boy

His first name was Ferdinand. But as a boy, his friends and family called him Pedro. He was born into a noble Portuguese family in 1480. The Magellan family had once been rich. It still owned lands here and there. But it no longer had a great deal of money.

Pedro's father had great hopes for his son. He hoped that Pedro would rise to a high post in the government. To pave the way, he got the boy placed as a page at the Portuguese court. Pedro learned he was to be page to the queen of Portugal. One might think that would be an honor. But it was not.

In fact, it was a lowly job. Pedro had to run errands. He had to clean the queen's rooms. He helped in the palace kitchens. He waited on tables. Worst of all, he was on call 24 hours a day. He was often waked in the middle of the night for some unimportant task. There was no point in complaining. There were many boys who would be more than happy to take his place.

The job did have one bright spot. A page was given a good education. He was taught to read and write and to do sums. He learned a bit of history. The study of geography did not take much time because little was known of the world outside of Europe.

Pedro's father knew many important men. These good friends liked Pedro and often took him home with them for a weekend. If Pedro had wanted to be given a high place at court when he grew up, they would have been glad to help. But from an early age the boy had other ideas. Very big ideas!

CHAPTER 2

Five Ships

Just 27 years had passed since Columbus discovered America. Now many men were eager to find other new rich lands. *Courage* was the key word. Life at sea could be a horror. Ships at that time were small. They did not have much space for food and water. Sailors looked on the wind as a friend. It had to blow them to a port before they died of hunger or thirst. They faced other dangers as well – storms, shipwrecks, rat-bite fever, getting lost at sea. It is a wonder that so many brave men dared to risk their lives on the high seas.

Pedro Magellan had grown into such a man. His dreams were the dreams of a man who wanted adventure and excitement. Even at court it had been clear that his life would not be like that of most men.

He was lucky. In those days a man could join the military service as both a sailor and a soldier. That is what Magellan did just as soon as he was old enough. He wanted to see the world. This seemed the best way to do it.

He chose wisely. Year after year he was sent to foreign lands. His nimble brain and courage made him stand out from the rest of the crowd.

He was still quite young when he was made a captain. In a battle with the Moors he suffered a painful leg wound. It left him lame for the rest of his life. But it did not slow him down!

Magellan had an idea. He thought it was a good one. He could not shake it. He wanted to find a new route to the East Indies. Such a search could not be done without money. Lots of money. He went to see the king of Portugal. The king listened and then said no.

Magellan would not give up. If not Portugal, why not some other country? He moved to Spain. He was quite sure that the Spanish people would like to find a new route to the East Indies. The only known route at that time was under the control of Portugal. A new route would mean that ships could reach the East Indies by sailing west instead of east through the waters of the southern tip of Africa guarded by Portuguese ships.

Why were the East Indies so important? Spices! They were in great demand all over Europe. And the East Indies were the main source of supply for many kinds of spice. Any ship loaded with spices was bound to bring its owners and crew a huge fortune.

The king of Spain said yes! Five ships and 270 men left Spain in the fall of 1519. The ships were the *Trinidad*, the *Santiago*, the *Concepcion*, the *Victoria*, and the *San Antonio*. The small fleet headed south and then due west. In time it

Magellan's Ships

reached South America and cruised down its eastern coast. Magellan explored every inlet. Somewhere there had to be a passage to a great ocean!

His crew worked hard. Each boring day was like the one before it. The food was bad and there was not much of it. The weather was cold and wet. And each inlet they followed came to a dead end. Then the ships had to turn back to the coast and start south again. The seamen and their officers were in low spirits. One day they began a mutiny. It did not last long. Enough men stood by Magellan to put down the uprising.

The next bitter blow came when one of the five ships, the *Santiago*, was wrecked. Now there were only four ships. Magellan was still full of hope. And one lucky day he found a channel between high steep cliffs. It was narrow and winding. The small ships were lashed by strong winds and rain.

On a dark night one of the ships, the *San Antonio*, turned and fled. It headed straight home to Spain. Now there were only three ships. It took them a month to sail from one waterway to another and then another. But at last success! The ships came to a huge ocean. The chain of waterways through which the ships sailed is still known as the Straits of Magellan.

Magellan was thrilled. At last they were on their way to the East Indies! He called for a day of feasting. He asked the ship's priest to lead the crew in prayer. He fired off the ship's guns to show his joy. He told his men fame and fortune would surely be theirs.

Not all agreed with him. The seamen thought they had done enough. They wanted to go home. The ship's astronomer was one who hated the thought of going on. The bitter cold made his bones ache. He tried to talk Magellan out of sailing at night. Sailing during the day held danger enough. Sailing at night – this was madness.

But Magellan was a stubborn man. He had found his ocean. Now he had to go on. Surely the worst was behind them. One of his officers wrote down the words Magellan had said that day. "We are now steering into waters where no ship has sailed before. May we always find them as peaceful as they are this morning. In this hope I shall name this sea the Pacific."

Would he have gone on had he known about the dark days that lay ahead?

CHAPTER 3

A Seaman's Life

We will halt the story of Magellan for a bit. It is time to speak of the brave men who sailed with him. And to tell of the hard life they led on board ship.

Times had changed. Now all kinds of men were eager to be seamen. Some went to sea to find new lands. Some went to escape going to prison. Some were seeking their fortune. Most were young. Some had been to sea before. Some had not. They were rough men who came from many countries. They all had one thing in common. They had no glimmer of what lay ahead.

Most ships had one young boy on board. It was his job to sing prayers at sunrise and sunset. There was a ship's carpenter to make repairs and a sailmaker to mend torn sails. A cooper kept barrels and tubs watertight. His job was an important one. The barrels and tubs held food and water. He had to check them often. Now and then the food or water looked as if it were about to spoil. Then it would have to be eaten or drunk at once. Nothing could be wasted.

The seamen were known as "able" or "ordinary." The able seamen worked on the ship's rigging high above the deck. The ordinary seamen scrubbed the deck and polished the brass. Then there were the officers – and, of course, the captain!

Every one of the crew knew one fact. They were never allowed to forget it. The captain was master of the ship. His word was law. He could be kind or he could be cruel. Before a voyage seamen prayed for a good master. He would control their lives as long as they were at sea.

Life at sea was humdrum. There was little to look forward to. The crew knew that the food on board ship would be plain fare. They hoped there would be enough of it. They were used to eating foods that kept well: dried beans, cheese, honey, nuts, sardines, raisins, and hard biscuits. The biscuits were known as hardtack. They were made of flour and water. Even when they were freshly made, the seamen didn't like them. And on long trips the hardtack sometimes crawled with worms. In those days a seaman had to have a strong stomach!

Food was cooked on an iron stove on deck. This was partly because of space but mostly for fear of fire. The stove was placed on the downwind side of the ship. This decreased the danger from sparks. Most food was boiled. The seamen ate it on deck. Their tablecloth was a piece of old sailcloth. It looked something like a picnic. But here were no sandwiches, pickles, cold drinks, or ants!

There was never enough space on the small ships. A man was not important but food and water were. And the cargo was the most important of all. So the men were jammed in a small space for sleeping. Not only was it small but often damp and dirty. Seamen were used to this but they never learned to like it. They spent as much time as they could on deck even when they were not on duty.

No matter what took place, the captains and crews in the 1500s had only themselves to rely on. A seaman had to be clever with his hands. He might not have on hand what he needed to fix an object that was broken. At such times he had to use his wits and make do with whatever he could find.

One thought haunted every man at sea. Suppose the ship was wrecked during a storm. They might be stranded on a strange shore. It might be a place no one had ever heard of. It would not appear on maps. No friendly ship was likely to sail by and pick them up. They might have to stay there for the rest of their lives. Or they might be caught and killed by natives.

The fear of disease was always present. Scurvy was the most common. It would be more than 200 years before Captain Cook of England found out how to prevent scurvy. Until then seamen all over the world had to put up with it –

and die of it. There was also the chance of typhoid when the water in the casks grew old and sour and full of germs. They feared typhus from the lice that crawled on dirty bodies and clothes. There was no doctor aboard ship in those days. So they had to rely on one another — and on their leaders. Even if a doctor had been on hand, it might not have done much good. The art of medicine still had far to go.

These, then, were the men who sailed with Magellan. Who fought beside him in the Philippines. Who stood beside him on storm-tossed decks. Who died in his service. We owe much to these unsung heroes.

CHAPTER 4

Three Ships

The sea had stayed calm. The weather stayed fair. Magellan had no way of knowing how huge the Pacific Ocean was. He did not know that it covered more than 64 million square miles. He had no clear maps to guide him. He did have a compass. He also used the stars.

For almost four months the little ships sailed on. Now there was a new problem. Supplies were running low. There was little food, and it was moldy and full of worms. The water was yellow and foul. Scurvy, the dreaded wasting disease caused by lack of fresh foods in the diet, struck the crew. They grew more and more hungry with each passing day. They ate leather rope guards, then sawdust, and even rats. Many died. The rest had lost hope.

At last the ships blundered onto the Mariana Islands. Such a relief! Now they had fresh food and water and time to care for the sick. But there were troubles even in this beautiful place. The natives were thieves. They jumped onto their outrigger canoes and paddled out to the ships. Once on board, they grabbed whatever they liked. Magellan tried to put up with this. After all, he thought, in a way they were like children. But the day came when he could stand it no longer. The islanders had stolen the longboat that was towed behind the *Trinidad*. Magellan had to have that longboat. It was used to explore coasts too shallow for the big ships.

He picked 40 of his strongest men. They rushed ashore and grabbed the longboat. It was time to teach the natives a lesson. The angry seamen burned huts and took all the food they could carry. Then the three ships pulled up anchor and left. Once again they sailed west.

In a week they reached the Philippine Islands. Magellan had learned his lesson. He wanted no trouble with any more natives. He searched for a small island with no people. Here the seamen set up camp. They raised one tent just for the sick and weak. Now Magellan could watch his men begin to get well and strong.

Of course, the Philippine islanders knew they were there. Time passed. Then one day the Spaniards and the natives made contact. Language might have been a problem but Magellan had a slave from Malay. The man could understand Tagalog, the language of the Philippines. He helped the two groups trade with one another. The islanders loved bells, mirrors, combs, and anything red. The sailors loved seafood and fresh fruit.

Magellan had only 150 men left. He felt he had to prove how superior they were. He may have wanted to show they were gods and could not be killed. He dressed a seaman in full armor. Then he told three other men to attack him with swords and clubs and knives. Of course, the man was unhurt. The islanders were amazed. They told their chiefs that one sailor was as strong as a hundred of their own people. The chiefs came to see for themselves. They liked what they saw. These were strong men who could win wars. Yet they seemed to be peaceful.

Now the men from Spain and the men from the Philippines were friends. Magellan moved his camp to a nearby island with lots of people. He soon learned that Christianity was unknown in the Philippine Islands. He thought it was his duty to tell the islanders about it. He was liked and respected so the natives were willing to listen to him. He had some small statues of the Christ Child. He gave them to the children. It looked as if this new religion might spread from one tribe to another. Magellan thought this would please the King of Spain.

The local chief was named Calambu. He said he would guide the ships to the Island of Cebu. There they could load up with food and other supplies. Then they could start again for the Spice Islands.

Cebu was quickly reached. Magellan made friends there with a chief who was called Humabon. The chief was spellbound by the

English weapons. First he was shown a crossbow, then strange sticks of wood that shot fire. He had never seen such things! These, he thought, would help him with his enemies.

Humabon asked Magellan to join him in an attack on a nearby island. Magellan was not sure this would be a good move. But Humabon would not give up. At last Magellan agreed. It turned out to be a tragic mistake!

Magellan had only 48 men against a force of 1,500 islanders. In the battle many of his crew were taken prisoner. Others were killed.

Magellan's small force was slowly driven back onto the beach and into the water. There on the shoreline Magellan was wounded in his arm.

Death of Magellan

He could not draw his sword to defend himself. A native slashed his left leg.

Later an officer wrote, "That caused the captain to fall face downward. Then they rushed upon him with spears and knives. They killed our mirror, our comfort, and our true guide."

CHAPTER 5

Two Ships

Their leader was dead. They were thousands of miles from home. In fact, the men of the *Trinidad*, *Victoria*, and *Concepcion* didn't know exactly where they were. And they didn't know what to do. One thing was clear. They needed to sail their ships away from the Philippines as fast as possible.

There was no one to take charge of the three battered ships. Each ship had its own captain. These men did their best. But they had never been leaders before so they made mistakes. They did not disagree with one another. It was mostly a case of not knowing where to go or how to get there. For six months the three ships drifted around the southern Philippines. Had they only known, they were less than three weeks of sailing time from the Spice Islands. The islands for which they had come so far and suffered so much!

As always there were problems. The worst problem was lack of men. Men had died in battle. Men had died of scurvy. Men had been taken prisoner. There were now only about 130 seamen left to man three ships. That was simply not enough.

The fleet pilot had an idea. One of the ships would have to be left behind. They talked about which one. The *Concepcion* was chosen. It was in the worst shape of the three ships. The crews set to work. They stripped the *Concepcion* of all useful cargo and supplies. Half of her crew went to the *Trinidad*. The other half went to the *Victoria*.

The two ships sailed on. At last one day in November 1521 they sighted the Spice Islands. It had been more than two years since they had set out from Spain.

The Spice Islands were now known as the Moluccas. One of the islands was called Tidore. It was ruled by a sultan. He was a cheerful, friendly man, and he liked the men from Spain. He was more than happy to trade with them. This was good news. The Spaniards knew that the sultans of some of the islands would trade only with the Portuguese.

The crews of the *Trinidad* and *Victoria* set to work with light hearts. They loaded the ships with cloves, cinnamon, nutmeg, and other rare spices. They dreamed of the riches their cargo would bring. They worked as fast as they could. There was no time to lose for the easterly windy season of the Indies had begun. Ships had to have an east wind at their backs to sail west around the Cape of Good Hope at the southern tip of Africa.

One officer wrote, "Our haste to get back to

Spain made us trade our goods to the natives for less than we should have gotten. But we wanted to be sure the wind was at our back on the voyage home."

At last the ships were loaded. Repairs had been made. Food and water had been stored. They were ready to leave. But then – another setback. The *Trinidad* had sprung a bad leak.

By this time the crews had come to respect Juan del Cano. He had been one of Magellan's officers. He seemed to be a strong leader. They knew Magellan had trusted him. Del Cano took a vote. It was agreed that the *Victoria* would leave at once. She did not have quite enough seamen. Thirteen young men from Molucca said they would join the crew. With 47 Spaniards, this would make a full crew.

Fifty-four men were left behind to repair the *Trinidad*. It would not be an easy job. Once she was shipshape, she would head *east*. With any luck she would be able to retrace the route Magellan had taken. Alas! These plans never came to pass. The *Trinidad* set out bravely. Bad weather, hunger, and scurvy drove her back to the Moluccas. Here the ship and its crew were captured by some Portuguese traders. They had fought bravely but they were weak and worn out. Only four members of the crew lived to tell the tale. And it took them years to make their way back to Spain.

The *Victoria* had set sail for Spain in December 1521. Juan del Cano was in command. No one knew what lay in store. All they knew was that the journey would be a long, hard one. Just how long and hard no one had any idea. And perhaps it was better that they did not know. The trip home was to be quite as grim as the first crossing of the Pacific.

CHAPTER 6

One Ship

Juan del Cano knew where he was going and how to get there. But he also knew he had to sail through seas controlled by the Portuguese. He dared not make a mistake and land on an African shore. There the crew could be arrested by the Portuguese. They would be thrown into prison at once. There would be no one to help them escape. Chances were they would never see home again. The need to steer clear of Portuguese warships added thousands of miles to the trip back to

Spain. It also made the trip longer by many months.

Del Cano stopped at a port in Indonesia for fresh food and water. Then he pointed the *Victoria* southwest. He sailed 3,500 miles across the southern Indian Ocean. In this way he could steer clear of the Cape of Good Hope and the Portuguese warships there. These enemy ships were ready to pounce on any Spanish ship that came nearby.

Time passed slowly. By March the crew of the *Victoria* was in bad shape. They had nothing to eat but rice. They had battled high seas and freezing gales for months. The foresail had been torn by a savage storm. This damage slowed the ship just when speed was important. Men were dying of hunger and scurvy.

At last the *Victoria* slipped by the Cape of Good Hope. Now the little ship could head north. But its troubles were far from over. Fewer than 30 men were still alive. They were too weak to sail the ship. Del Cano had no choice. He had to steer for the Cape Verde Islands off the coast of Africa. These islands were held by the Portuguese. But his men were dying. Del Cano had to get food for them.

The hull of the ship was worm-eaten. It leaked like a basket. The foremast was gone. Much of the ship's rigging was rotten. Repairs had to be made before the *Victoria* could go on.

At first the Portuguese were friendly. They even helped the *Victoria's* crew put up a new foremast.

Del Cano tried to trick them. He told them that the ship was on its way back from America. He said they had been driven off course by a storm. It almost worked. But then a seaman from the *Victoria's* landing party was caught with a package of cloves in his pocket. The secret was out! It was clear that the ship had come from the East Indies. The 13 men in the landing party were flung into jail. Del Cano made plans for the *Victoria* to leave as fast as he could. Up the anchor! Back to sea went the run-down ship for the last lap of its rugged journey.

At last in September 1522 the *Victoria*

reached the coast of Spain. The voyage to the East Indies and back had taken three years. Del Cano did not stop. He sailed his ship up the river to Seville. Two hundred and seventy men had left Spain three years earlier. Only 18 of them came back. One crew member wrote, "We sailed 43,380 miles. We circled the world."

The seamen left the ship. They knelt and kissed the soil of Spain. The whole city of Seville crowded to see these brave men. They were hailed as heroes. But in one way the crowd was shocked. The men were bone thin. Their cheeks were hollow. Their clothes were in tatters. The poor diet had caused many to lose teeth and hair. The crowd roared its welcome anyway. The men

The Victoria

who had put up the money for the voyage rushed forward. They wanted to shake hands with the men who had made them rich.

The *Victoria* brought 26 tons of spices home. They were sold for a huge profit. Enough profit was made to pay for the entire three-year voyage. Not much was left over. At least not enough for the seamen. They did not get the riches Magellan had promised. Del Cano fared somewhat better. He was given a small pension.

Why has Magellan been given credit for being the first man to sail around the world? After all, it was del Cano who brought the *Victoria* home to Spain. There are many reasons for Magellan's fame. And they all ring true.

First, the idea to sail *west* to the East Indies was his. He worked hard for years to make such a voyage happen. Second, he sailed farther west than any man before him. He crossed a point sailing west that people had only reached sailing east. His log revealed the true size of the Pacific. He gave Spain a hold on the Philippines with the new westward route.

He brought back knowledge of the world and its peoples never known before. He made it possible for other men to use that knowledge to explore new lands. Within 100 years of his death, the route he charted through the oceans opened trade routes never thought of before.

Sadly, Magellan and most of his men never

knew what a gift they had made to Spain and to the rest of the world.

It was Magellan's dream that started other men dreaming.